flute

Now you can be the feature flute soloist on eight specially recorded arrangements

TAKE
THE
LEAD

flute

D0416344

THE BLUES BROTHERS

IMP

International MUSIC Publications

International Music Publications Limited
Griffin House 161 Hammersmith Road London W6 8BS England

Series Editor: Sadie Cook

Editorial, production and recording: Artemis Music Limited
Design and production: Space DPS Limited

Published 1999

International MUSIC Publications

© International Music Publications Limited
Griffin House 161 Hammersmith Road London W6 8BS England

International Music Publications Limited

England: Griffin House
161 Hammersmith Road
London W6 8BS

Germany: Marstallstr. 8
D-80539 München

Denmark: Danmusik
Vognmagergade 7
DK1120 Copenhagen K

Carisch

Italy: Via Campania 12
20098 San Giuliano Milanese
Milano

Spain: Magallanes 25
28015 Madrid

France: 20 Rue de la Ville-l'Eveque
75008 Paris

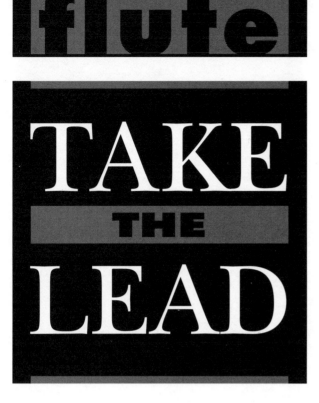

flute

TAKE THE LEAD

In the Book...

n the CD...

Demonstration   Backing

She Caught The Katy And
Left Me A Mule To Ride

Words and Music by
Taj Mahal and Yank Rachel

Demonstration   Backing

Gimme Some Lovin'

Words and Music by Steve Winwood,
Muff Winwood and Spencer Davis

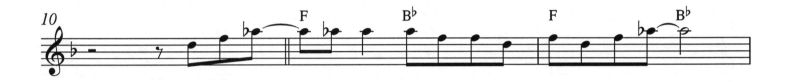

Everybody Needs Somebody To Love

Words and Music by Bert Berns,
Solomon Burke and Jerry Wexler

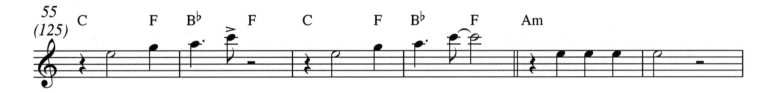

Demonstration   Backing

Shake A Tail Feather

Words and Music by Otis Hayes
Andre Williams and Verlie Rice

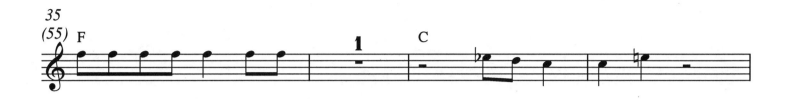

The Old Landmark

Demonstration   Backing

Words and Music by Adeline M Brunner

Brightly

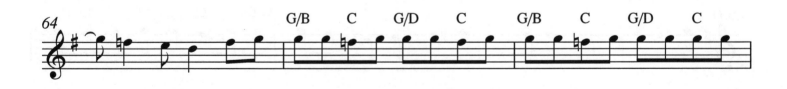

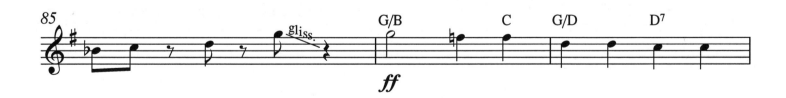

Think

Words and Music by
Ted White and Aretha Franklin

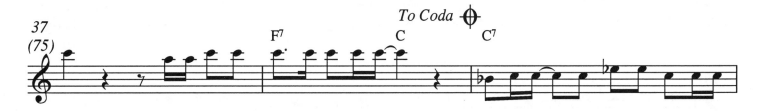

To Coda

D.S. al Coda

CODA

Minnie The Moocher

Words and Music by Cab Calloway,
Irving Mills and Clarence Gaskill

Slower

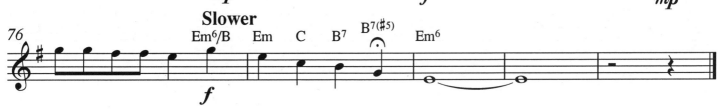

Sweet Home Chicago

Words and Music by Robert Johnson

Demonstration   Backing

10/99

Reproduced and printed by
Halstan & Co. Ltd., Amersham, Bucks., England